WiSH BOARD

The visualisation panel is a tool of successful people

Ash Boni

The visualisation panel is a tool of successful people

In order to achieve our goals and dreams, we need to take advantage of the law of attraction and the law of visualisation, and the vision board helps us do this. The wish board refers to your personal vision and desires.

The wish board is a collection of images or objects arranged to help you in the manifestation process. You can create a wish board for a longer or shorter period, depending on your goals. A very common technique is to make this vision board annually.

Visualisation is powerful for the brain

The wish board is an amazing tool for goal setting and vision creation, it's to help you focus and manifest what you want to attract into your life. If you have decided to make a wish board you surely know and understand what you want and what you choose to create in your life.

This journal will help you to make your wish board, go through all the materials you have created (images, texts) and look for what you feel matches the emotions you want. Arrange them without thinking too much about a predefined order. Let your intentions work for you! Focus on emotion, feeling, soul.

Don't forget to write down a deadline for each one until you want your wish to come true. But be realistic in your choice of date, so as not to be disappointed when it doesn't happen "on time".

When you create a visiualisation board and place it somewhere you'll see it every day, you're more likely to achieve your goals.

If you've made your board start working towards achieving your desires, analyse your habits, see what obstacles you need to overcome, get organised. It's not enough to just make the board and wait for the wishes to come true.

Periodically review your priorities. From time to time, revisit your wishes and re-examine them, see what their status is and if your priorities are the same.

How can you create your own wish board?

1. Clarify your intentions

2. Gather your materials

- large sheet of cardboard / cork board / notebook / notice board

- glue / thumbtacks
- scissors
- magazines / books / listed sheets from which to cut out the relevant pictures; when choosing the pictures, bear in mind that you are not just putting up pictures, but that the pictures should create a positive emotional state when you look at them.

3. Put the board in a visible place

4. Start working towards your goals

Good luck in creating your wish board and making it come true !

GOALS

Family

holiday planning
quality time
family activities
periodic phone calls
family dinner
visits of parents

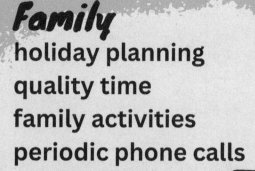

Education

read daily
personal development
getting motivated
new courses
economies
expense accounting

Love

free program synchronization
romantic holiday planning
communication
couple activities

Health

healthy eating
daily sport
sufficient relaxation
reduced stress
daily water needs
regular medical check-ups

Friends

Periodic exits
communication and support
regular phone calls
board games
shows
trips

Business

relationship development
membership
online shop
trainings
turning hobbies into business
participation in training courses
and conferences

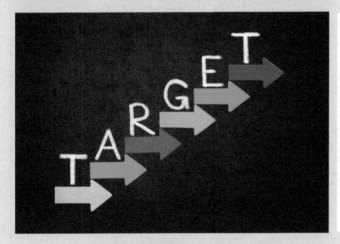

My Dream

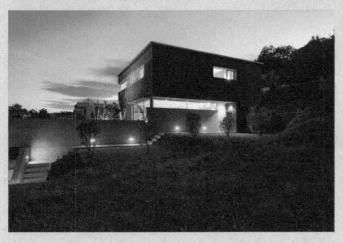

PRIZE
$ 1,000,000

Investments

T Together
E Everyone
A Achieves
M More

A ACTION
C CHANGES
T THINGS

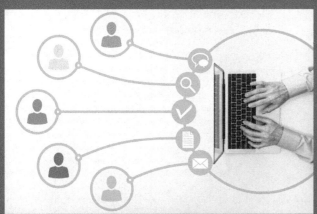

WORK FROM HOME

train
info
learn
study
class
skill
Workshop
seminar

PRIORITY IMPORTANT

Coaching Goal Collaboration
Training TEAM BUILDING Support
Skill Solution Motivation

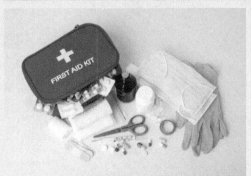

My passions/ hobbies

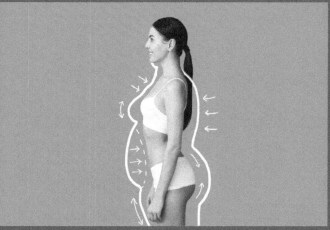

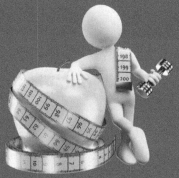

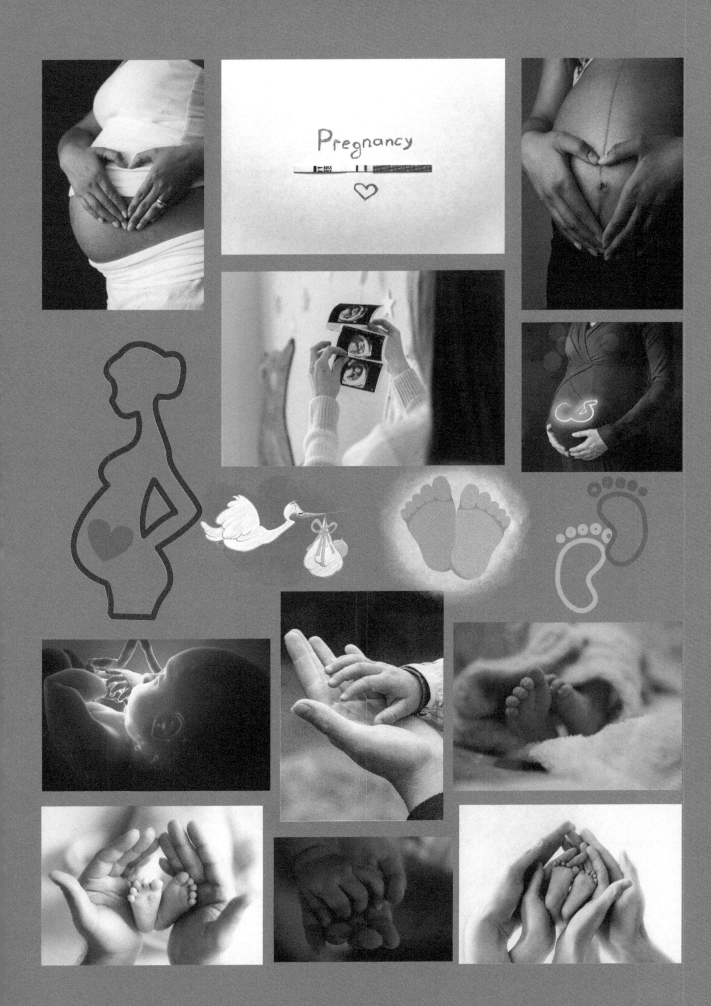

Pregnancy

BEST
FRIENDS
♥ ♥ ♥

DUBAI   JAPAN   ITALY

PARIS   CANADA   CHINA

PRAGUE   BERLIN   GREECE

EUROPE   AFRICA   MOSCOW

NEW YORK   MALDIVES

CUBA   POLAND   CROATIA

MONACO   SPAIN   BRAZIL

SWEDEN   USA   PORTUGAL

GERMANY   DENMARK

IRELAND   ROMANIA

MALTA   CHICAGO   MEXIC

MONTREAL   LAS VEGAS

Don't be busy, be efficient and productive.

A long journey starts with the first step.

Be the energy you want to attract.

SUCCESS

Great accomplishments are not born out of your comfort zone.

DON'T BE AFRAID OF FAILURE

I can & I will

YOU ARE STRONG

IT WILL BE HARD BUT NOT IMPOSSIBLE

Don't stop dreaming

Trust yourself

Lives the present!

ACCEPT CHANGE

Now or ne er

dream

DON'T GIVE UP

Think positive

You have to keep going

You're doing better than you think

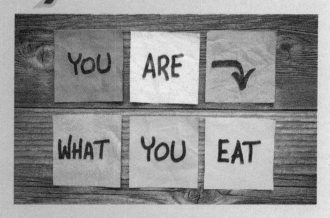

YOU ARE ✓
WHAT YOU EAT

Good VIBES

MINDSET IS EVERYTHING

ENJOY TODAY

YOU ARE IMPORTANT

Smile EVERYDAY

LOVE MYSELF

I CAN -and- I WILL

STAY STRONG

Don.t be afraid to be Great

DREAM BIG

DO WHAT YOU LOVE

be kind YOURSELF

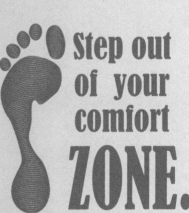

Step out of your comfort ZONE.

Vision board

2023

2024

2025

2026

2027

DREAM BIG

2028

2029

2030

Believe *in* yourself

RESTART

Thank you.

We hope you enjoyed our book.

As a small family company, your

feedback is very important to us.

Please let us know how you like

our book at:

ashboni739@gmail.com